$\mathcal{T}$HE STAR *of* BETHLEHEM

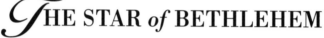

THE STAR *of* BETHLEHEM

The History, Mystery, and Beauty
of the Christmas Star

JEANNE K. HANSON

ILLUSTRATIONS BY GLENN WOLFF

HEARST BOOKS · NEW YORK

This book is dedicated to my grandparents. —JH

The author is indebted to three astronomers for the richness of fact in this book:
Owen Gingrich, astronomer and historian of science at the Harvard-Smithsonian Center
for Astrophysics, whom I interviewed for a magazine story on this subject; David Hughes,
astronomer at the University of Sheffield (England), whose book *The Star of Bethlehem*
(see bibliography) can be heartily recommended for all its great detail; and Karlis Kaufmanis,
astronomer emeritus at the University of Minnesota, whose Christmas speech on the
Star of Bethlehem has been heard by more than 600,000 people, including me.

It is the policy of William Morrow and Company, Inc., and its imprints and affiliates,
recognizing the importance of preserving what has been written, to print the books we publish
on acid-free paper, and we exert our best efforts to that end.

Library of Congress Cataloging-in-Publication Data

Hanson, Jeanne K.
The star of Bethlehem: the history, mystery, and beauty of the Christmas star/
by Jeanne K. Hanson; illustrations by Glenn Wolff.
p.   cm.
Includes bibliographical references.
ISBN 0-688-13120-4
1. Star of Bethlehem. 2. Bible. N.T. Matthew II, 1-10—
Criticism, interpretation, etc.   I. Title.
BT315.2.H33 1994
232.92—dc20   94-5509
CIP

Printed in the United States of America

First Edition

1 2 3 4 5 6 7 8 9 10

BOOK DESIGN BY GLENN WOLFF & LAURIE DAVIS

$\mathcal{C}$ONTENTS

THE STORY of the STAR

Long ago, a star shone…

$\mathcal{N}$ow when Jesus was born in Bethlehem of Judea in the days of Herod the king, behold, there came wise men from the east to Jerusalem, saying, Where is he that is born King of the Jews? for we have seen his star in the east, and are come to worship him. When Herod the king had heard these things, he was troubled and all Jerusalem with him. And when he had gathered all the chief priests and scribes of the people together, he demanded of them where Christ should be born. And they said unto him, In Bethlehem of Judea: for thus it is written by the prophet, And thou Bethlehem, in the land of Juda, art not the least among the princes of Juda: for out of thee shall come a Governor, that shall rule my people Israel.

Then Herod, when he had privily called the wise men, enquired of them diligently what time the star appeared. And he sent them to Bethlehem, and said, Go and search diligently for the young child; and when ye have found him, bring me word again, that I may come and worship him also. When they had heard the king, they departed; and, lo, the star, which they saw in the east, went before them, till it came and stood over where the young child was. When they saw the star, they rejoiced with exceeding great joy. And when they were come into the house, they saw the young child with Mary his mother, and fell down, and worshipped him: and when they had opened their treasures, they presented unto him gifts; gold, and frankincense, and myrrh. And being warned of God in a dream that they should not return to Herod, they departed into their own country another way.

— MATTHEW 2:1-12

No more detail than this is offered. The star is not mentioned at all in the gospels of Mark, Luke, and John. The New Testament Bible was formed by the early church over a period of three hundred years, during which time church leaders pondered what was important and what authentic. Along the way, a book called the Protoevangelium of James was written, but it was decided that it should not be included in the Bible. The book does, however, mention the Star of Bethlehem, and the author stresses its brightness. This is all the original material about the shining star that we have in words.

What is this Star of Bethlehem? A beautiful enigma, it has thrown its light down the centuries.

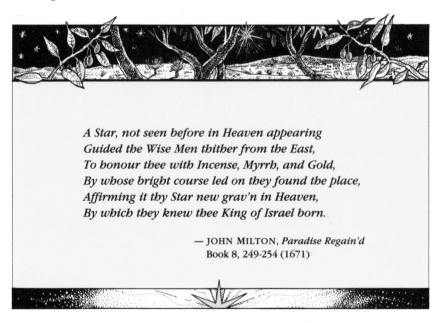

A Star, not seen before in Heaven appearing
Guided the Wise Men thither from the East,
To honour thee with Incense, Myrrh, and Gold,
By whose bright course led on they found the place,
Affirming it thy Star new grav'n in Heaven,
By which they knew thee King of Israel born.

— JOHN MILTON, *Paradise Regain'd*
Book 8, 249-254 (1671)

Black Sea

Caspian Sea

MEDIA

ASSYRIA

BABYLONIA
BABYLON

Mediterranean Sea

PERSIA

Persian Gulf

JERUSALEM
BETHLEHEM
Dead Sea

AFRICA

ARABIA

River Nile

Red Sea

EARLY IDEAS

Whence comes this rush of wings afar,
Following straight the Noel star?
Birds from the woods in wondrous flight,
Bethlehem seek this Holy Night.

—"Carol of the Birds"
Traditional

tars appeared elsewhere as signs in ancient times. In his epic poem *The Aeneid*, Virgil showed a star guiding the hero Aeneas to the site where Rome should be built. In the Hebrew tradition, a star appears occasionally to persuade the people to listen to warnings, to shine in announcement of the birth of Moses, to alert the Israelites that a tyrant would try to kill Abraham. In what is called the Jewish "midrashic tradition," a priestly way of understanding, the religious and the poetic mingle thus.

Also in ancient days, people tried hard to divine ways in which the New Testament fulfilled the old. They pondered Old Testament passages like these:

> *There shall come a Star out of Jacob, and a Sceptre shall rise out of Israel.* — NUMBERS 24:17

> *The morning stars sang together, and all the sons of God shouted for joy.* — JOB 38:7

> *Canst thou bind the sweet influences of Pleiades, or loose the bands of Orion?* — JOB 38:31

> *He telleth the number of the stars; he calleth them all by their names.* — PSALMS 147:4

> *The heavens declare the glory of God; and the firmament showeth his handiwork.* — PSALMS 19:1

But the Star of Bethlehem is no mere literary device, though it may well have these overtones in tradition. Were it midrash or prophecy fulfillment alone, the story in Matthew would be more elaborate, more focused on the past prophecies, much more formulaic; midrash and prophecy are handled in these ways elsewhere in the Bible.

One must ponder a central question: Was the star a miracle? A natural object? Both? Historians, astronomers, all of us have wondered. Let us look at the story, the mystery, behind the Star of Bethlehem in more detail before deciding, each of us according to personal beliefs.

Johannes Kepler, a great and devout astronomer of the seventeenth century, was the first to consider the Star of Bethlehem carefully in this way. He had been watching the ordinary stars and planets of mid-December 1603 when the planets Jupiter and Saturn began to move closer together. In the almost-Christmas sky, their slow minuet lasted ten days, though they never came close to touching (even from our viewpoint on Earth). Kepler knew about planetary motions, of course, and he realized that these dances of approach are not rare; astronomers call them "conjunctions." But still, he thought again about the story in the Bible.

By late 1604, another sky event happened before Kepler's eyes and near the same two planets. It was a supernova, a star explosion. In light of his knowledge of astronomy, Kepler came to this understanding of the Star of Bethlehem: To make its Christmas light, two planets had come close. Then, through the grace of God, they had ignited a nearby star to explode. All three heavenly bodies had flung

their light across the ancient sky in honor of Christ's birth.

But this is not a firm answer to our star's mystery. Though no one in Kepler's time knew it, the planets and the stars are light-years apart. Nor do planets have fire of their own with which to ignite another heavenly body. They shine only with the Sun's reflected light. And how could even a bright cluster of planets or stars lead the Wise Men, then hover over a place of birth?

The first Noel the angels did say
Was to certain poor shepherds in fields as they lay:
In fields where they lay keeping their sheep
On a cold winter's night that was so deep.

Noel, Noel, Noel, Noel,
Born is the King of Israel

They looked up and saw a star
Shining in the east beyond them far,
And to the earth it gave great light.
And so it continued both day and night.
   Chorus
And by the light of that same star,
Three wise men came from country far,
To seek for a King was their intent.
And to follow the star wherever it went.
   Chorus
This star drew nigh to the northwest,
O'er Bethlehem it took its rest,
And there it did both stop and stay
Right o'er the place where Jesus lay.
   Chorus

Then enter'd in those wise men three,
Full reverently upon their knee,
And offer'd there in His presence,
Their gold and myrrh and frankincense.

   Chorus

     —"The First Noel"
      Traditional (sixteenth century)

O little town of Bethlehem,
How still we see thee lie;
Above thy deep and dreamless sleep
The silent stars go by:
Yet in thy dark streets shineth
The everlasting Light;
The hopes and fears of all the years
Are met in thee tonight.

For Christ is born of Mary;
And gathered all above,
While mortals sleep, the angels keep
Their watch of wond'ring love.
O morning stars, together
Proclaim the holy birth;
And praises sing to God, the King,
And peace to men on earth.

    —PHILLIPS BROOKS and LEWIS H. REDNER
    "O Little Town of Bethlehem" (1865)

⅁HE WISE MEN

At the end we preferred to travel all night,
Sleeping in snatches,
With the voices singing in our ears, saying
That this was all folly.

—T. S. ELIOT, "The Journey of the Magi" (1927)

Near Herod's Palace. As Gabriel dis-
appears, all is Darkness, save a Star
in the East. Enter First King, riding,
his eyes upon the Star. He is black
and of great stature. Attendants.

FIRST KING JASPER.
Lord, of whom this light is lent,
And unto me this sight has sent,
I pray to thee, with good intent,
    From shame me shield;
So that I no harmes hent[1]
    By fell or by field.

Also I pray thee specially,
Thou grant me grace of company
That I may have some solace by,
    In my travail[2]:
And, certes, for to live or die
    I shall not fail,

Till that I in some land have been,
To wit what this Starne may mean,
That has me led, with beames sheen
    For my cuntre;
Now wend I will, nor doubt, I ween,
    The sooth[3] to see.

Enter Second King, Melchior, riding
and attended. He is of little stature.

MELCHIOR.
Ah! Lord, that is withouten end!
Whence does this selcouth[4]
light descend,
That thus so kindly has me ken'd[5]
    Out of my land,
And showed me where I may attend,—
    Thus bright shinand[6]?

Certes, I saw never none so bright;
I shall not rest by day nor night,
Till I wit whence may come this light,
    And from what place.—
He that it sent unto my sight
    Lend me that grace!

JASPER. *[Accosting the Second King.]*
Ah, sir, whither are ye away?
Tell me, good sir, I you pray.

MELCHIOR.
Certes, I trow, the sooth to say,
    None wot but I.—
I have followed yon Starne, veray,
    From Araby;

For I am king of that cuntre
And Melchior there men call me.

[1]receive [2]laborious journey [3]truth
[4]wondrous [5]called [6]shining

JASPER.
And king, sir, was I wont to be,
    In Tars, at hame[7],
Both of town and of city;
    Jasper is my name;

Yon Starne's light shone to me thither.

MELCHIOR.
That lord be loved that sent me hither!
For it will straightway guide us whither
    That we shall wend.
We owe to love him both together,
    That it to us wold send.

Enter the Third King, Balthasar,
attended, gazing upon the Star.
He is of middle size.

BALTHASAR.
Ah, Lord! in land what may this mean?
So selcouth sight was never seen,
Such a Starne shinand so sheen,
    Saw I never none;
At once it lightens all between,
    By him alone.

What it may mean, that know I naught;
But yond are two, methink, in thought,—

[Approaching the other Magi.]
I thank him that them hither
has brought
    Thus unto me:—
I shall assay if they wot aught
    What it may be.

Lordings, that are lief[8] and dear,
I pray you tell me with good cheer
Whither you wend, in this manere,
    And where that you have been;
And of this Starne that shines thus clear,
    What it may mean.

JASPER.
Sir, I say you certainly,
From Tars for yon Starne sought have I.

MELCHIOR.
To seek yon light from Araby,
    Sir, have I went.

BALTHASAR.
Now heartily I thank him for-thy,[9]
    That it has sent.

—Medieval Miracle Play
    "The Star of Bethlehem"
    Scene i

[7]home   [8]welcome   [9]therefore

he Wise Men are the part of the Star of Bethlehem story closest to our human experience. They have been a template for our imaginations for centuries. Were they truly kings, resplendent in golden robes and bearing jeweled boxes brimming with precious gifts, as they have been shown since the days of medieval literature and art? Were there, indeed, even three of them? They must be a mirror held up to our own respect, our own belief that only royalty is worthy to be first visitors. The Bible, however, says no such thing.

The account in Matthew calls them "wise men," not kings. And nowhere is the number "three" offered, nor are any names for them provided.

To know who the Wise Men might truly have been, one must discern something of their historical context. In the lands and kingdoms of two thousand years ago that are now known as the Middle East, a "wise man" was a priest.

Throughout that part of the world at about the time Christ was born, the priests and the people were awaiting a Messiah. Hope was strong that a holy leader would come to redeem the world. This strain of religious expectation was strong in the Jewish tradition, but Jews were not alone. A feeling was in the air, one that would have made the priests of all religions watchful.

Not every ancient priest watched stars in the sky, of course. Nor would most of them have contemplated a long journey to follow a star, considering it an important sign. The Wise Men of the story in

Matthew were probably among that class of priests who had a deep knowledge of the stars and planets, of astrology. Historians think that they were probably Zoroastrian priests.

In those days, the center for the study of astrology was in Babylonia. And astrology was a blend of all that was known about astronomy with what we now define as astrology. The priests who studied it were among the most learned men of their time, careful students of the sky. They kept precise records of the movements of the planets against the constellations of the zodiac, with an emphasis on the planets. This emphasis evolved because planets move in more complicated ways, at least from our earthly viewpoint, while the stars describe the same bright circles.

These Babylonian records, kept by priests like the Wise Men, are

consulted by astronomers even today; they look at them for accurate historical records of a comet's much earlier appearance, for example.

Centers for priestly study in the ancient world were also set in Media, Persia, Assyria and Arabia. But there were fewer Jews in those places to keep messianic expectations especially strong in the minds of the priests.

Probably Zoroastrian priests from Babylonia, the Wise Men would have been considered significant messengers. And they often visited kings. Their procession to Herod by camel was not unusual. The Wise Men's knowledge was considered so deep as to be part magic by the people of the time, and, in fact, the word "magic" has its derivation in the name they were called: The Magi.

To these men, a star rising in the East was of great importance.

'A cold coming we had of it,
Just the worst time of the year
For a journey, and such a long journey:
The ways deep and the weather sharp,
The very dead of winter.'
And the camels galled, sore-footed, refractory,
Lying down in the melting snow.
There were times we regretted
The summer palaces on slopes, the terraces,
And the silken girls bringing sherbet.
Then the camel men cursing and grumbling
And running away, and wanting their liquor and women,
And the night-fires going out, and the lack of shelters,
And the cities hostile and the towns unfriendly
And the villages dirty and charging high prices:
A hard time we had of it.
At the end we preferred to travel all night,
Sleeping in snatches,
With the voices singing in our ears, saying
That this was all folly.

Then at dawn we came down to a temperate valley,
Wet, below the snow line, smelling of vegetation;
With a running stream and a water-mill beating the darkness,
And three trees on the low sky.
And an old white horse galloped away in the meadow.
Then we came to a tavern with vine-leaves over the lintel,
Six hands at an open door dicing for pieces of silver,
And feet kicking the empty wine-skins.
But there was no information, and so we continued
And arrived at evening, not a moment too soon
Finding the place; it was (you may say) satisfactory.

All this was a long time ago, I remember,
And I would do it again, but set down
This set down
This: were we led all that way for
Birth or Death? There was a Birth, certainly,
We had evidence and no doubt. I had seen birth and death,
But had thought they were different; this Birth was
Hard and bitter agony for us, like Death, our death.
We returned to our places, these Kingdoms,
But no longer at ease here, in the old dispensation,
With an alien people clutching their gods.
I should be glad of another death.

—T. S. ELIOT, "The Journey of the Magi" (1927)

$\mathcal{R}$ISING *in the* EAST?

One star differeth from another star in glory.

—I CORINTHIANS 15:41

I n Matthew's Gospel, the Star of Bethlehem appears "in the east." This part of the mystery leads us to a rather arcane point of biblical translation. The Bible was written in classical Greek, the international language of the world known to the people of the Middle East. In that language, the word for "in the east" in its singular form also means "opposite the Sun." In such an "acronychal rising," a star moves from east to west across the sky for the whole night. And it also offers an important insight into *this* particular star, since otherwise "in the east" could characterize half the stars in the sky. (It was not at all unusual for ancient stories to speak with some vagueness about matters like this.)

A star that rises opposite the Sun would have been considered especially important by the Magi of those times. They thought that it would influence later events. So the Wise Men who saw such a star would watch it even more closely than other heavenly bodies.

But what was this star?

Some say that ever 'gainst that season comes
Wherein our Saviour's birth is celebrated,
The bird of dawning singeth all night long;
And then, they say, no spirit can walk abroad;
The nights are wholesome; then no planets strike,
No fairy takes, nor witch hath power to charm,
So hallow'd and so gracious is the time.

—WILLIAM SHAKESPEARE, *Hamlet*
Act I, scene i (ca. 1601)

I kiss my hand
To the stars, lovely-asunder
Starlight, wafting him out of it; and
Glow, glory in thunder;
Kiss my hand to the dappled-with-damson west:
Since, tho' he is under the world's splendour and wonder,
His mystery must be instressed, stressed;
For I greet him the days I meet him, and bless when I understand.

—GERARD MANLEY HOPKINS, "The Wreck of the
Deutschland, Part the First," Stanza 5 (1918)

*H*EROD *the* KING

...Now when Jesus was born in Bethlehem
of Judea in the days of Herod the King...

—MATTHEW 2:1

erod, known as Herod the Great in the histories of his time, knew that a Messiah was expected by his people. Even before his father, Antipater, had appointed him king of Galilee, he had lived in Judea, now Israel, and knew the hopes of the Jews.

A supremely powerful man and a keen politician, Herod usually acted quickly and decisively. Outlaws who threatened his borders on the Syrian frontier were put to death. So were rivals suspected of conspiracy. And, after siding with Antony, who lost to Caesar in the dominant Roman politics of the era, Herod courted Caesar's favor so astutely, his own crown in hand, that he became the Roman emperor's trusted governor and friend.

Once secure yet again, Herod turned to public works that were popular with the people. He restored the Jews' Temple to "a magnificence never surpassed," according to the historian Josephus. He rebuilt one coastal town in white stone, with palaces. For other towns in his realm he constructed new walls, new marketplaces, new halls, even gymnasia. Herod brought to his subjects stability, prosperity, and peace; after entertaining Caesar at a banquet, he even received more territory to govern.

This is not a man who would want a rival "King of the Jews" to arise. Already he had ordered the death of John the Baptist. Herod wanted his own dynasty to continue, although he was worried about his future even without a Messiah present, since there was discord among the children of his first and second wives.

This is certainly a man whom the Magi would visit. They would consult with him about happenings in his sphere of power.

Herod was neither priest nor astronomer, and this helps us to understand the Star of Bethlehem. The star must have been a sky phenomenon of some subtlety; it must have been something that the Magi would recognize as important but that others, even Herod himself, might know to exist but not see as significant. After all, in the Bible story, Herod had to be told about the star in detail by the Wise Men.

The star must have been a rather long-lived phenomenon, too. Herod saw the need to order the death of all children in his realm under the age of two years, not knowing which were born under the auspicious star. This was surely a broad and unpopular edict from a ruler who otherwise sought strong favor.

*A*nd when they were departed, behold, the angel of the Lord appeareth to Joseph in a dream, saying, Arise, and take the young child and his mother, and flee into Egypt, and be thou there until I bring thee word: for Herod will seek the young child to destroy him. When he arose, he took the young child and his mother by night, and departed into Egypt: And was there until the death of Herod: that it might be fulfilled which was spoken of the Lord by the prophet, saying, Out of Egypt have I called my son.

Then Herod, when he saw that he was mocked of the wise men, was exceeding wroth, and sent forth, and slew all the children that were in Bethlehem, and in all the coasts thereof, from two years old and under, according to the time which he had diligently inquired of the wise men. Then was fulfilled that which was spoken by Jeremiah the prophet, saying, In Rama was there a voice heard, lamentation, and weeping, and great mourning, Rachel weeping for her children, and would not be comforted, because they are not.

But when Herod was dead, behold, an angel of the Lord appeareth in a dream to Joseph in Egypt, saying, Arise, and take the young child and his mother, and go into the land of Israel; for they are dead which sought the young child's life. And he arose, and took the young child and his mother, and came into the land of Israel. But when he heard that Archelaus did reign in Judea in the room of his father Herod, he was afraid to go thither: not withstanding, being warned of God in a dream, he turned aside into the parts of Galilee: And he came and dwelt in a city called Nazareth: that it might be fulfilled which was spoken by the prophets, He shall be called a Nazarene.

—MATTHEW 2:13-23

𝒯WO IMPORTANT DATES

*Yet a little while is the light with you. Walk while
ye have the light, lest darkness come upon you.*

—JOHN 12:35

erod's reign itself provides more insight into the Star of Bethlehem, since his death is one of two dates that must frame its appearance. Herod the Great is known to have died by the spring of 4 B.C.; after that date, of course, he could not have met with the Magi or issued any murderous orders. We know from biblical chronology, too, that the rising of the star occurred rather late in his reign.

The second date that frames the star is the decree of Caesar Augustus "that all the world should be taxed." Herod carried out all the orders of Caesar in his part of the realm. And Caesar's rule extended from 31 B.C. to A.D. 14. That decree is what drew Mary and Joseph to Bethlehem. From historical accounts we know that it was probably issued in 8 B.C.

It seems, then, that the Star of Bethlehem shone between 8 B.C. and 4 B.C. Its light changed the sky and made the Magi undertake the journey by camel from Babylonia to Jerusalem, then Jerusalem to Bethlehem. Early church leaders, who lacked the historical records we now have, placed its appearance closer to the year zero in their estimates.

Saint Stephen was a clerk in King Herod's hall,
And served him with bread and cloth, as every king doth befall.

Stephen out of kitchen came with boar's head in hand;
He saw a star was fair and bright over Bethlehem stand.

He cast adown the boar's head and went into the hall.
"I forsake thee, King Herod, and thy workes all."

"I forsake thee, King Herod, and thy workes all;
There is a child born in Bethlehem is better than we all."

"What aileth thee, Stephen? what is thee befall?
Lacketh thee either meat or drink in King Herod's hall?"

"Lacketh me neither meat nor drink in King Herod's hall;
There is a child born in Bethlehem is better than we all."

"What aileth thee, Stephen? art thou mad or raving indeed?
Lacketh thee either gold or fee or any rich weed?"

"Lacketh me neither gold nor fee nor any rich weed;
There is a child born in Bethlehem shall help us in our need."

"That is as sooth, Stephen, all as sooth, ywis,
As this capon shall crow that lieth here in my dish."

That word was no sooner said, that word in that hall,
That capon crew "Christus natus est!" among the lords all.

"Rise up, my tormenters, by two and by one,
And lead Stephen out of this town and stone him with stone!"

Then took they Stephen and stoned him in the way,
And therefore is his eve on Christ's own day.

—"Saint Stephen and Herod"
(mid-fifteenth-century ballad)

If thou follow thy star, thou canst not fail
of a glorious haven.

—DANTE, *The Inferno of the Divine Comedy*
Canto XV (1321)

$\mathcal{W}$HAT COULD *the* STAR BE?

He telleth the number of the stars,
he calleth them all by their names.

—PSALMS 147:4

he Star of Bethlehem has been sought for centuries, and to dispel its mystery, people have suggested almost every phenomenon of the sky: comets, meteors, ball lightning, the zodiacal light, the northern lights, novae, supernovae, variable stars, and various planets. The Bible story in Matthew is so evocative, yet innocent of detail, that the mystery of the star may never be clearly solved. But since we have already delved a bit into early ideas about the star, the Wise Men, the rising in the east, and Herod the Great, we can at least narrow the range of sky phenomena that could have produced it. Let us look at each of them.

A comet could have led the Magi to Bethlehem, since a bright-tailed "star" like this can easily be visible for several months. A comet can even be seen in two stages, which fits with the Bible story since it allows the star to appear to the Wise Men over a long period of time: Comets streak toward the Sun, disappear when they are close to it, and then can reappear, catching the Sun's light as their path swings them out deep into the solar system again. Comets have long been both feared and marveled at, their apparitions recorded carefully by ancient Chinese, Babylonian, and Korean scholars. For this reason, we know that the black of the Middle Eastern sky was broken by comets in 146 B.C., 12-11 B.C., and 5-4 B.C., the appearances closest to Jesus' birth. The second of these comets was visible for two months, the third for a somewhat shorter period of time. Indeed, the comet of 5-4 B.C. fits, though only roughly, with the decree of Caesar Augustus.

But comets do not move the way the Star of Bethlehem is said to move, since they do not "rise in the east." And the Magi would not have considered a comet as portentous as a planetary happening, since they could not then predict comet appearances. (Predicting them can be difficult even today.) Nevertheless, a significant minority of astronomers are inclined to think that this comet of 5-4 B.C. was the Star of Bethlehem.

❈

Was the Star of Bethlehem a meteor? Large meteors are often called falling stars since they fall toward the earth (unlike comets, which continue to orbit the Sun). Though they are not stars, meteors can be very bright. And a meteor can indeed fall toward a particular place. But meteors flash for a few seconds only, perhaps a moment or two if the chunk of rock and metal is particularly large. A star described as one that "stays before" the Magi must have lasted at least the hour and a half it took in those days to travel from Jerusalem to Bethlehem. So a meteor does not seem to fit the rest of the star story as we know it. Several meteors would have been necessary, and unusual ones, carefully orchestrated in stages and falling in the same sky trajectory.

Ball lightning, so rare that very few people have ever seen it, has also been suggested as the Star of Bethlehem. Though meteorologists are still not quite clear about its origins, ball lightning is usually a multihued sphere of bright lightning. It may be as small as a marble or as large as a house. It does indeed move, sometimes briskly and sometimes almost hovering.

Farewell, Morning Star, herald of dawn,
and quickly come as the Evening Star,
bringing again in secret her whom thou takest away.

—MELEAGER (first century B.C.)

Thou fair-hair'd angel of the evening,
Now, whilst the sun rests on the mountains, light
Thy bright torch of love; thy radiant crown
Put on, and smile upon our evening bed!
Smile on our loves, and, while thou drawest the
Blue curtains of the sky, scatter thy silver dew
On every flower that shuts its sweet eyes
In timely sleep. Let thy west wind sleep on
The lake; speak silence with thy glimmering eyes,
And wash the dusk with silver. Soon, full soon,
Dost thou withdraw; then the wolf rages wide,
And the lion glares thro' the dun forest:
The fleeces of our flocks are cover'd with
Thy sacred dew: protect them with thine influence.

—WILLIAM BLAKE, "To the Evening Star" (1783)

But this strange force lasts for only a very short time, from a few
seconds up to a couple of minutes. It does not seem that it could lead

the Magi or impress them with its astrological significance.

Another suggestion centers on the zodiacal light, a beautiful blur in the sky visible to careful observers just after sunset. This light is created when the Sun, slightly below the horizon after sunset, shines up onto astronomical and earthly dust particles, always seen more thickly on the horizon (since we are looking through more layers of them there). Though the zodiacal light can be about as bright as the Milky Way, which is in fact not very bright, and though planets can appear embedded in it, which adds to its glow, it was probably too ordinary a phenomenon to have driven the Magi from their desks. Remember that in those days the sky was much darker than it is now and the zodiacal light probably quite common; we, on the other hand, are bathed in our own pools of electrical light.

Venus also has been mentioned as a possible Star of Bethlehem, perhaps in its conjunction, or sky approach, with Jupiter in 3 B.C. or 2 B.C., when both were seen in the constellation Leo. These known dates, however, do not fit with Herod's death, nor would that sky location have been particularly important to the Magi.

❖

Northern lights are beautifully ephemeral, yet persistent. This kind of light might seem to "go before" the Magi and "stand over" Bethlehem, since a sky dance of northern lights may last for hours, then reappear the next night or even for several nights in conspicuous display. Made by the invisible energy of the Sun's solar wind as it hits Earth's magnetic field, the northern lights can blur the night sky with pale green, white, even red, each color the characteristic light of an atmospheric gas ionized (or stripped of electrons) high in the sky. The light sways, coruscates, ripples, dances. Exquisitely common at sub-Arctic and Arctic latitudes (with their mirror images deep in the Southern Hemisphere), northern lights are extraordinarily rare as far south as Israel, where they would arise in the north (not the east) if at all. Had such a rare and ethereal display occurred there, ancient astronomers probably would have recorded it. It is not likely that the Magi would have considered the northern lights a sign of a Messiah.

❄

Another phenomenon suggested as a possible Star of Bethlehem is a nova. A kind of stellar explosion, a nova happens when a star is brightened suddenly by an event on its surface. This flaring can make a star that once appeared ordinary flame ten thousand to one hundred thousand times its usual brightness. The quickening usually lasts for one or two months. Novae are not rare in our galaxy: About fifty such events occur each year, with a couple of these close enough to be visible through a telescope. However, a nova visible to the naked eye would be seen only once every generation or so, even in the very dark skies of the biblical era.

Astronomical records, especially the Chinese "Twenty-four Histories," show that a nova explosion indeed brightened a faint star in 5 B.C., though not dramatically to the eye. A few astronomers

There was a star danced, and under that was I born.

—WILLIAM SHAKESPEARE, *Much Ado
About Nothing*, Act II, scene i (1598)

*I see thy glory like a shooting star
Fall to the base earth from the firmament.*

—WILLIAM SHAKESPEARE, *Richard II*
Act II, scene iv (1595)

*Our birth is but a sleep and a forgetting:
The soul that rises with us, our life's Star
Hath had elsewhere its setting,
And cometh from afar:
Not in entire forgetfulness,
And not in utter nakedness,
But trailing clouds of glory do we come
From God, who is our home:
Heaven lies about us in our infancy!*

—WILLIAM WORDSWORTH
"Ode: Intimations of Immortality from
Recollections of Early Childhood"
Stanza 5 (1806)

think that this might have been the Star of Bethlehem. The nova would not have moved in any unusual way, however, and the Magi would have considered it of only average importance.

Could the star have been a supernova instead—a star explosion that is radically more violent than a nova? Not merely a surface explosion, this rarer event happens when an aged star becomes unstable, then explodes entirely. Most of its matter is strewn into space. A supernova is about one thousand times brighter than even a nova and is visible in this altered state for a period lasting from a week or two up to a couple of months or so. But there are no records of any such dramatic happening, visible to the naked eye, at the time. Had a supernova appeared in the sky, the ancient scholars certainly would have noted it.

A "variable star" may be a more likely candidate for the Star of Bethlehem. From ancient records we know that two such stars came to brightness at about the time of Christ's birth. Variable stars naturally change in brightness, without the kinds of violence endured in nova and supernova explosions. The star Mira, in the constellation Cetus, is variable, as are three stars in the constellation Cassiopeia. One of the latter was indeed considered to be related to Syria and Palestine astrologically. Although a minority of astronomers believe one of these variable stars to be a possible Star of Bethlehem, even they admit that these stars are not much brighter in their bright phase than in their subtle phase, from our vantage point on Earth.

The Star of Bethlehem might conceivably have been Venus, our ordinary "neighborhood" planet, but clad in brightness. Just as the Moon seems to go through phases, from half Moon to full Moon and so on, from our viewpoint on Earth, so does Venus. Further, the differing swings of Venus and Earth around the Sun sometimes bring us closer together than at other times. A "full" Venus especially close to Earth is so bright that even today astronomy departments at universities and the local planetarium get phone calls when Venus shines this way. "What *is* that in the sky?" people ask.

There is no doubt that the brightest Venus would be noted by Jerusalem's populace. But whether its light would have drawn the Magi to their journey is another matter. Just a few scholars believe this to be our star.

It is also possible that the Star of Bethlehem was simply a miracle, an event beyond nature created by God to signal the birth of Jesus.

But just as much reverence may be felt when considering yet one more natural sky event.

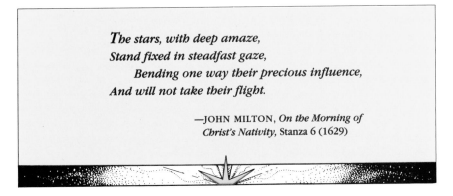

The stars, with deep amaze,
Stand fixed in steadfast gaze,
* Bending one way their precious influence,*
And will not take their flight.

—JOHN MILTON, *On the Morning of Christ's Nativity,* Stanza 6 (1629)

$\mathcal{A}$PPROACHING *the* MYSTERY

The day star arise in your hearts.

—II PETER 1:19

sky object held, convincingly, to be the Star of Bethlehem must meet several tests: It must have appeared, and significantly, to the Wise Men before they started a journey, then continued to be evident to them as they planned and took their trip. It must have been a phenomenon so unusual and so important in terms of their learned expectations that they decided to travel all the way to Herod the King in Jerusalem, then to Bethlehem. It must also have been an event that occurred at the right time. Caesar's decree in 8 B.C. and Herod's known death by early 4 B.C. must frame this event, the Star throwing its light across the sky between these two dates. It must have gone unnoticed by Herod until the Wise Men told him about it. And it must have somehow seemed to "go before" the Magi and then "stand over" Bethlehem.

These requirements, taken together, immediately suggest to most astronomers one kind of heavenly body: planets. Because of the path of Earth against the sky's black-velvet background, the planets, and not the stars, appear to move most variously. (Stars are beyond the Sun, so far away that they merely make great arcs.)

And there is one planetary phenomenon recorded by ancient astronomers that seems to meet the requirements for the Star of Bethlehem.

This phenomenon is recorded in the star almanac of Sippar, a Babylonian record written in cuneiform. The sky happening was a conjunction, or coming together, of planets that began in 8 B.C. and continued into 6 B.C. Conjunctions are artifacts of our vantage point on Earth. A pair of planets or a planet and the Moon appear to be close, though one is actually in the foreground and the other in the background. If they are two planets, they are millions of miles apart, but to our eyes they seem to line up. If the pair is a planet and a star, again, they seem to line up, although the two are actually many light-years apart: The planet is in our solar system and the star far beyond.

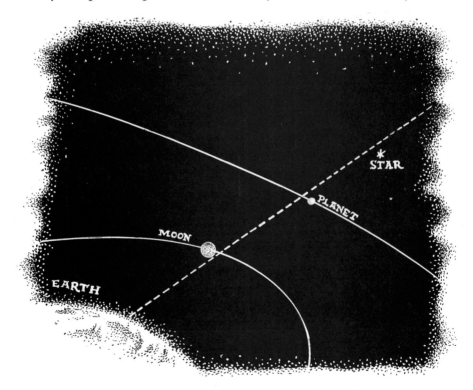

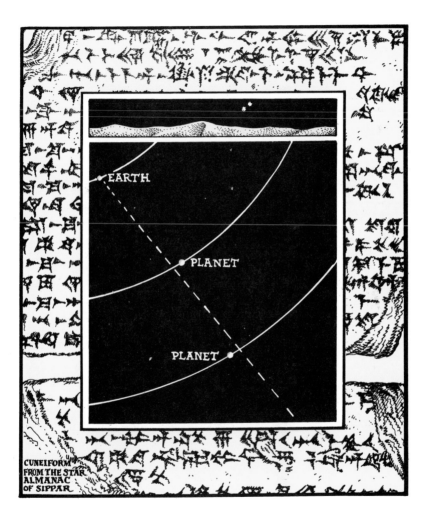

EARTH

PLANET

PLANET

CUNEIFORM
FROM THE STAR
ALMANAC
OF SIPPAR

$\mathcal{A}$ DANCE of PLANETS

*The morning stars sang together, and
all the sons of God shouted for joy.*

—JOB 38:7

he planet dance that made the music of the Star of Bethlehem story was probably a minuet in three stages, with Jupiter and Saturn mingling their light three times and Mars joining at the end.

In late 8 B.C., Jupiter and Saturn began to approach each other quickly in the sky. To the Magi, this was not unusual, since a planetary conjunction of some kind occurs several times a year in the skies of Earth. But this conjunction was especially interesting, and they would have been watching its development closely for three reasons: In their learned system, Jupiter was the symbol of a king and of God, Saturn was a sign for the Jewish people and the Messiah, and the central part of the constellation Pisces, where the planets appeared, was the Magi's symbol of the House of David and Palestine. This conjunction was also a dawn rising "in the east," which to them meant a birth.

Shining even over the glare of our cities' electric bonfires today, Jupiter is bright. Saturn is dimmer, but it can be seen easily with the naked eye in all but a few of our largest cities today. When the two planets seem close together, it is evident that Jupiter moves faster (because its orbit lies closer to the Sun than Saturn's). They seem, then, to be in a sky race. At the first rising of Jupiter in the 8 B.C. conjunction, it was closer to the Earth and thus especially bright. Saturn was seen tilted partly on its end with the rings blurred, adding their light. In the ink-black skies of biblical days, this conjunction would have been a truly impressive sight.

The conjunction became even more dramatic by early 7 B.C. when Jupiter and Saturn, which had been rising in the east, set together close to the Sun as it, too, slipped below the horizon. So both planets seemed to flare bright just as they became visible. (They were not visible at all, of course, while the Sun's full light flooded the sky.) Then, quickly, it was the planets' time to set and they disappeared.

❋

No one knows at what time the Magi left their homes, probably in Babylonia, to call upon Herod in Jerusalem. But once they saw and pondered the conjunction, planning such a trip would take at least a few weeks, and getting there would consume three or four months. Camels are not quick animals.

The conjunction continued. After passing behind the Sun, and so becoming invisible from our vantage point on Earth, Jupiter and Saturn appeared together again by the spring of 7 B.C. They rose with the Sun now instead of setting with it. This made them bloom very briefly just before sunrise, when the Sun overwhelmed their light. By May they were yet closer together and shining at night again. And in July both Jupiter and Saturn seemed to stop in the sky, since their orbital speeds differ from ours on Earth.

Late in 7 B.C. the sky dance took two new, important, turns. The planet Mars began to join Jupiter and Saturn, and Jupiter seemed to pause again while it approached Saturn more closely. Jupiter and Saturn were close in early October and again in early December. Since

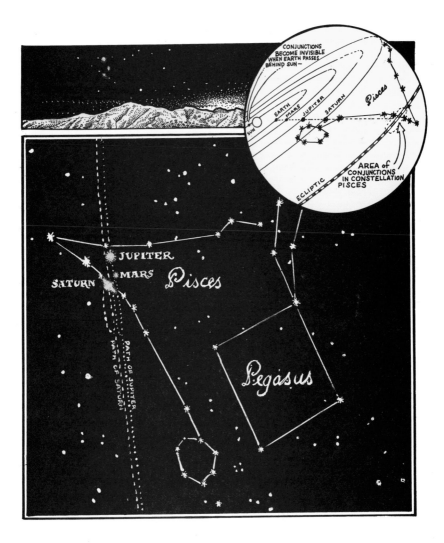

CONJUNCTIONS
BECOME INVISIBLE
WHEN EARTH PASSES
BEHIND SUN—

SUN EARTH MARS JUPITER SATURN

Pisces

ECLIPTIC

AREA of
CONJUNCTIONS
IN CONSTELLATION
PISCES

JUPITER

SATURN MARS Pisces

PATH OF JUPITER
PATH OF SATURN

Pegasus

Mars is nearer the Sun than both its giant planetary cousins, it moves even faster than they do and would have seemed to be winning a heavenly race toward the end of that year.

The three planets became close sky companions again by early 6 B.C. They also set together, joining the Sun. The triple conjunction was thus complete: three close approaches of Jupiter and Saturn, with Mars very near, too.

By the spring of 6 B.C., the planets' paths were widening again. The conjunction was over.

In this dance Jupiter and Saturn had come together three times, with Mars quick to appear and catch them in sky flight—an event that happens only once every 805 years. For the conjunction to begin in the constellation Pisces, the sign of the House of David, is rarer yet. This has occurred just three other times in nearly three thousand years.

The conjunction itself is not in doubt. Babylonian priests recorded it in cuneiform, Chinese astronomers noted it, and an Egyptian record on papyrus mentions it. The Magi would have recognized it, once it began, since planetary motion tables were quite advanced in those days. Johannes Kepler, the seventeenth-century astronomer, worked backward from a similar 1604 conjunction, knowing well that such conjunctions occurred every 805 years somewhere in the sky; he also extrapolated further back to suggest a date for the birth of Moses and even of Adam.

A recently suggested variant on the triple-conjunction hypothesis centers on Jupiter alone. In late September of 5 B.C., Jupiter seemed to pause in the sky, from the viewpoint of those on Earth. This stillness happens only once every 399 days. Although the Magi would have known of the regular nature of this event, they still recorded it in their cuneiform writings.

The three-stage dance of planets, however, is most likely to be what we know and love as the Star of Bethlehem.

THE STAR'S IMPORTANCE

It ended ...
With his body changed to light,
A star that burns forever in that sky.

— *The Flight of Quetzalcoatl* (Aztec god),
  a Mexican myth

*M*ystery yet remains. Our heavenly minuet never looked like a single star: Jupiter and Saturn were never closer together than two full-Moon widths. The light of Mars did not seem to fuse with their brightness, either. And the Bible story speaks of a "star," not "stars" or "planets."

But certainly the whole phenomenon of the planetary conjunction could have been thought of as a single miraculous occurrence, not only by the people of the day but by later biblical writers. Layers of time and tradition have made the Star of Bethlehem story yet more blurred but also more powerful. We, too, think of it as a single sky event, and one to follow somehow.

Like the Magi, we have sought the Star. In Christmas carols, in poems, in song and pageant, we search for the Star of Bethlehem each year. We ponder it and wonder at it. The Star that fills our imaginations has never been reduced to simplicity. It shines still.

Bright star, would I were stedfast as thou art—
Not in lone splendor hung aloft the night
And watching, with eternal lids apart,
Like nature's patient, sleepless Eremite,
The moving waters at their priestlike task
Of pure ablution round earth's human shores.

—JOHN KEATS, "Bright Star" (1820)

*J*N CELEBRATION

The Stars shined in their watches, and rejoiced.

—I BARUCH 3:34

The Star of Bethlehem will call to us always, in carols and in words…

At last surrounds their sight
A globe of circular light,
 That with long beams the shamefaced Night arrayed;
The helmed cherubim
And sworded seraphim
 Are seen in glittering ranks with wings displayed,
Harping loud and solemn quire,
With unexpressive notes, to Heaven's new-born Heir.

Such music (as 'tis said)
Before was never made,
 But when of old the sons of morning sung,
While the Creator great
His constellations set,
 And the well-balanced world on hinges hung,
And cast the dark foundations deep,
And bid the weltering waves their oozy channel keep.

Ring out, ye crystal spheres,
Once bless our human ears,
 If ye have power to touch our senses so;
And let your silver chime
Move in melodious time;
 And let the bass of heaven's deep organ blow;
And with your ninefold harmony
Make up full consort to th' angelic symphony.

   —JOHN MILTON, "On the Morning of
   Christ's Nativity," Stanzas 11-13 (1629)

The Christ-child lay on Mary's lap,
   His hair was like a light.
(O weary, weary were the world,
   But here is all aright.)

The Christ-child lay on Mary's breast,
   His hair was like a star.
(O stern and cunning are the kings,
   But here the true hearts are.)

The Christ-child lay on Mary's heart,
   His hair was like a fire.
(O weary, weary is the world,
   But here the world's desire.)

The Christ-child stood at Mary's knee,
   His hair was like a crown,
And all the flowers looked up at him,
   And all the stars looked down.

       —GILBERT KEITH CHESTERTON
        "A Christmas Carol" (1915)

We three kings of Orient are,
Bearing gifts we traverse far
Field and fountain, moor and mountain,
Following yonder Star.
Oh, star of wonder, star of might,
Star with royal beauty bright,
Westward leading, still proceeding,
Guide us to thy perfect light.

—JOHN H. HOPKINS, JR.
"We Three Kings of Orient Are" (1857)

The Messiah will come as soon as the most unbridled
individualism of faith becomes possible—when there is no one
to destroy this possibility and no one to suffer its destruction....
The Messiah will come only when he is no longer necessary;
he will come only on the day after his arrival; he will come,
not on the last day, but on the very last.

—FRANZ KAFKA, "The Coming of the Messiah"
from *Parables and Paradoxes* (1935)

Angels from the realms of glory,
Wing your flight o'er all the earth;
Ye who sang creation's story,
Now proclaim Messiah's birth:
Come and worship, Come and worship,
Worship Christ, the new-born King.
Sages, leave your contemplations,
Brighter visions beam afar;
Seek the great Desire of nations,
Ye have seen His natal star:
Come and worship, come and worship,
Worship Christ, the new-born King.

—JAMES MONTGOMERY (1816)
and HENRY SMART (1867)
"Angels from the Realms of Glory"

And there were in the same country shepherds abiding in the field, keeping watch over their flock by night. And, lo, the angel of the Lord came upon them, and the glory of the Lord shone round about them; and they were sore afraid. And the angel said unto them, Fear not: for, behold, I bring you good tidings of great joy, which shall be to all people. For unto you is born this day in the city of David a Saviour, which is Christ the Lord. And this shall be a sign unto you; Ye shall find the babe wrapped in swaddling clothes, lying in a manger. And suddenly there was with the angel a multitude of the heavenly host praising God, and saying, Glory to God in the highest, and on earth peace, good will toward men.

And it came to pass, as the angels were gone away from them into heaven, the shepherds said one to another, Let us now go even unto Bethlehem, and see this thing which is come to pass, which the Lord hath made known unto us. And they came with haste, and found Mary and Joseph, and the babe lying in a manger. And when they had seen it, they made known abroad the saying which was told them concerning this child. And all they that heard it wondered at those things which were told them by the shepherds. But Mary kept all these things, and pondered them in her heart. And the shepherds returned, glorifying and praising God for all the things that they had heard and seen, as it was told unto them.

—LUKE 2:8-20
"The Adoration by the Shepherds"

$\mathscr{B}$IBLIOGRAPHY

Barrett, C. K. *The New Testament Background: Selected Documents.*
New York: Harper & Row, 1961.

Freitag, Ruth S. *The Star of Bethlehem: A List of References.*
Washington, D.C.: Library of Congress, 1979.

Gayley, Charles Mills. *The Star of Bethlehem: A Miracle Play of the
Nativity.* New York: Fox, Duffield and Company.

Hughes, David. *The Star of Bethlehem: An Astronomer's Confirmation.*
New York: Walker and Company, 1979.

Johnson, Pegram III, and Edna Troiano. *The Roads from Bethlehem:
Christmas Literature from Writers Ancient and Modern.* Louisville, Ky.:
Westminster/John Knox, 1993.

Quarterly Journal of the Royal Astronomical Society, December 1992.